Woof and Welcome!

Hey there, human pups! I'm Bean, the beagle with a nose for adventure, and this waggy-tailed wonder is my best bud, Decker, the red-furred cocker spaniel with a tuft on his head that just won't behave!

We've sniffed out some pretty pawsome stories for you. Ever wonder what happens when you mix a beagle's curiosity with a spaniel's sass? Well, you're about to find out!

Our Tail-Wagging Tales
From chasing our tails to getting them caught in some hilariously hairy situations, we've got stories that will make you bark with laughter. Imagine trying to bake a cake with paws – yep, it was a frosting disaster! Or that time we thought we could be detectives like Sherlock Bones. Spoiler alert: sniffing out clues is harder than it looks!

A Nose for Fun
We love exploring, whether it's the great outdoors or the mysterious under-the-bed realm (spoiler: it's mostly dust bunnies). And, oh boy, do we have tales to tell! Like the Great Squirrel Chase of Sunday afternoon or the Mystery of the Missing Socks.

Paws and Reflect
But it's not all zoomies and chaos. We've learned some pretty cool stuff too, like the importance of friendship, sharing your treats (even though it's REALLY hard), and always, always having each other's backs.

Join the Pack
So, pull up a comfy cushion, grab your favorite chew toy, and get ready to embark on some tail-wagging adventures with us. We promise it'll be a howling good time!

With lots of licks and love,
Bean & Decker

P.S. Don't forget to check for squirrels before reading. They're sneaky little critters! 🐾 📚 🐶

Get ready for a festive whirlwind with "Bean and Decker's Moonlit Christmas Dash!" Join our beloved duo, Bean the beagle and Decker the red cocker spaniel, in an unforgettable Christmas Eve adventure. As the world sleeps, Bean and Decker embark on a thrilling moonlit escapade through frosty woods, meeting playful deer and even Santa Paws himself! They dive into a magical game, chasing a shimmering ball under the sparkling snow, filling the night with barks of joy. But the fun doesn't end there - Santa Paws whisks them away on a breathtaking flight, soaring over moonlit landscapes. This charming tale, brimming with laughter, snowflakes, and holiday magic, is a secret kept between Bean, Decker, and you. It's a Christmas story like no other, capturing the spirit of adventure and the joy of friendship. "Bean and Decker's Moonlit Christmas Dash" is a heartwarming read for the holiday season, perfect for kids and dog lovers alike!

Index

Zoom-Arooo Kids Club welcome letter .... page 9
Zoom-Arooo Poem .... page 11
Letter from Bean & Decker .... page 13
Bean & Decker's adventures – Moonlit Christmas Dash page 17
Bean & Decker's adventures - Holiday Heist .... page 23
Barks, Baubles, and the Beagle-Spaniel Christmas Boogie!   27

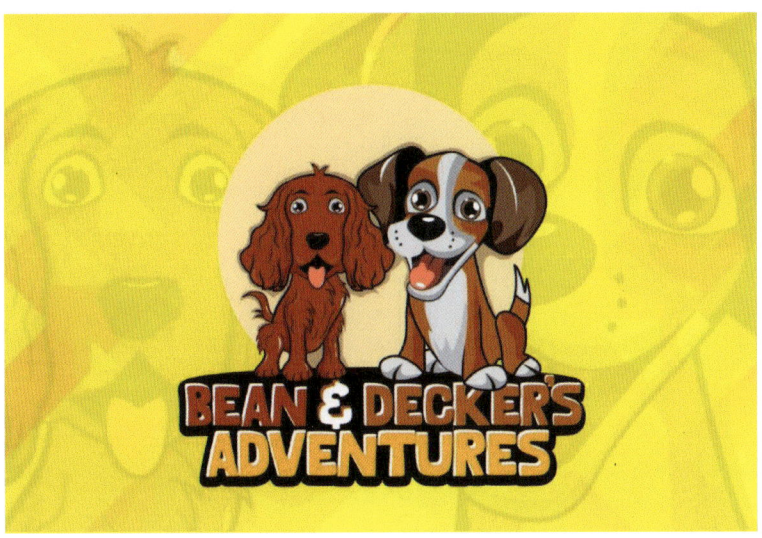

Dear Adventurer,

Congratulations and a tail-waggin' WELCOME to the Zoom-Arooo Kids Club! 🐾 ✨

You've just sniffed out the most pawsome club on the planet, where the grass is green, the sky's the limit, and every day is a barking good time. Bean the beagle and Decker the red cocker spaniel are wagging with excitement to share their most sniff-tastic adventures with YOU!

As a member of the Zoom-Arooo Kids Club, you'll emBARK on magical journeys with our furry friends. You'll giggle at Bean's hilarious hound antics and cheer as Decker unleashes a whirlwind of spaniel surprises!

But hold onto your hats, because there's more! 🎩

Each adventure is a chance to earn your very own PAW PRINT STAMPS! These aren't just any stamp, oh no - they're a sign that you've sniffed, wiggled and giggled through challenges just like our mystery-solving, tail-chasing duo!

How do you earn these Paw Stamps, you ask? By using your noggins, tickling your funny bones, and most importantly, by letting your imagination off the leash! With every story of Bean and Decker, you'll solve puzzles, uncover secrets, and laugh until your sides shake like a doggy drying off!

So lace up your adventure shoes, grab your explorer's cap, and get ready to zoom-a-rooo through tales taller than a Great Dane and more fun than a bucket of puppies!

Keep your whiskers twitching for your first adventure pack, arriving faster than Bean chasing a squirrel! It's packed with secret maps, giggles, and your very first mission!

Are you ready to roll? Bean's bouncing, Decker's dancing, and we can't wait to start this adventure with YOU!

On your marks, get set... ZOOM-A-ROOO!

Yours in adventure and tail wags,
The Zoom-Arooo Kids Club Team

The Zoom-Arooo Kids Club Poem

Welcome to the club where the fun never ends,
Zoom-Arooo Kids Club, where you'll find furry friends!
With Bean the Beagle, and Decker the Spaniel,
Adventures await that are truly sensational!

Put on your cap, tie those shoelaces tight,
Prepare for the giggles that last into the night.
Through jungles of backyard, or under the bed,
Where tales of tail wags are eagerly spread.

We zoom, we whoosh, we dart and we dash,
Through stories and puzzles, we're a merry mad mash.
With stamps to earn and new games to play,
In the Zoom-Arooo Kids Club, it's never a dull day!

Bean's antics will have you rolling on the floor,
While Decker's surprises leave you begging for more.
From magical mysteries to treasures unseen,
You're part of the pack, you're on the dream team!

So here's to the kids who love a good roam,
With Bean and Decker, you're never alone.
Zoom-Arooo Kids Club, it's more than a hoot,
It's the bark of excitement, the pursuit of loot!

In this club, we're brave, we're bold, we're clever,
Our stories and fun, they go on forever.
So welcome, new buddies, get set for a dive,
In the Zoom-Arooo Club, where imaginations thrive!

With each thrilling venture, with each wondrous tale,
Together we'll conquer, together we'll sail.

Onward to fun, where we all are the star,
With Zoom-Arooo spirit, we'll always go far!

Hey Zoom-Arooo Kids Club Pals!

🎄 🐾 🎁 Woof-Hoo! It's your fur-riends, Bean the Beagle and Decker the red Cocker Spaniel, writing to you from the coziest, most sparkle-filled corner of the living room, right under the Christmas tree (it's our secret clubhouse for now)!

We're wagging our tails off with excitement to tell you all about the most paws-itively amazing holiday adventures we've had—and guess what? We want YOU to join in on our festive fun!

🌟 ✨ The Great Cookie Caper! 🍪 ✨ 🌟
First up, we sniffed out a mystery worthy of the Zoom-Arooo Detective Stamp! The Case of the Vanishing Christmas Cookies! Spoiler alert: they were delicious—uh, we mean, the case is still unsolved. 😊 We need your super sleuthing noses to track down the clues and find the cookie culprit!

🎶 🎵 Sleigh Bells and Belly Rubs! 🎵 🎶
Next, we practiced our best howls and harmonies for the Zoom-Arooo Carolling Contest. Bean's howl is so beautiful it makes the ornaments jingle! Get ready to sing your hearts out and spread cheer that can be heard all the way to the North Pole!

🐕 🎈 Fetch the Festivity! 🎈 🐕
And who could forget the Zoom-Arooo Holiday Fetch Championship? We've been training in the snow, perfecting our sprints and leaps, and we can't wait to see how far you can zoom and swoosh to fetch that special, glittery holiday ball!

🏆 🥇 A Very Merry Race! 🥇 🏆
Hold onto your Santa hats, because we've saved the best for last! It's the Zoom-Arooo Jingle Bell Race! Can you dash faster

than Rudolph flies? Can you hop higher than the elves' tallest toy stacks? Show us your zoomiest moves and let's find out!

So, dear friends, as the stars twinkle and the snowflakes swirl, put on your most jolly jumpers, tie up your fastest sneakers, and join us for a Christmas filled with giggles, games, and good times. We can't wait to see you!

Lickety-split, let's make this the merriest, most unforgettable Christmas ever! We're already bouncing with anticipation to play and celebrate with each and every one of you.

Biggest tail wags and happiest woofs,

🐶 Bean and 🐕 Decker

P.S. Don't forget to bring your brightest smile and your loudest laugh—it's the secret ingredient for the perfect Zoom-Arooo Christmas, and keep practicing the Bark, Baubles and the Beagle-Spaniel Christmas Boogie song! 🎅 🤸

Bean and Decker's Moonlit Christmas Dash

Alright, Zoom-Arooo Kids, buckle up for the tail-wagging, snow-chasing adventure of Bean the beagle and Decker the red cocker spaniel in "Bean and Decker's Moonlit Christmas Dash!"

On Christmas Eve, when all the humans were snoozing, Bean and Decker couldn't even think about dozing! Their doggy hearts were thumping, and their noses twitched for fun, because Christmas meant toys and games and runs!

Bean's tail was a wiggly white brush, and Decker's coat shone like the fire's warm flush. They didn't want to sleep—not at all! So they made a plan, soft and small.

"Psst, Decker," Bean's whisper was sneaky and sly, "Let's have a midnight adventure, you and I!"

Decker's ears perked up, and his eyes sparkled bright. "An adventure? Oh, yes! What a brilliant night!"

Like little ninjas in the night, they slipped out the door—Bean and Decker were ready to explore! The moon was a big, shiny ball in the sky, lighting up the woods where secrets lie.

Their four paws crunched on the frosty ground. They zoomed through the trees, round and round! The woods were twinkling, mysterious and deep, and the tall trees seemed to peep.

Suddenly, rustle, rustle! What's that? Deer friends appear with a tip and a tap! Bean woofed hello, wagging her tail. Decker joined in; their friendship never fails! The deer, with a nod and a prance, danced away, making the most of their Christmas Eve stay.

Bean and Decker dashed through the snow, chasing each other and the moon's soft glow. They zoomed down hills and jumped logs big and stout, their doggy hearts filled with Christmas cheer, no doubt!

Then, what's that jingling in the air? A "Ho, ho, ho!" filled the square! Santa Paws was here, so big and merry, his sleigh parked nearby, his reindeer enjoying a berry!

"Hello, little pups! What fun you must seek! Let's play a game before you sneak back to sleep!" Santa Paws chuckled, his eyes a-twinkle. "A magical game? Give me a wink or a wrinkle!"

Out came a ball, shiny and bright, changing colours with every flight. Bean and Decker leaped high and low, catching the ball in the sparkling snow. They laughed and barked, their tails a blur—oh, what fun they had with her!

But all games must end, and Santa Paws knew, it was time for these pups to bid adieu. "Let's fly you home, my brave little pair. We'll zoom through the sky, through the cold Christmas air!"

With a flick and a swish of his magical reins, they soared over houses, fields, and plains. Bean and Decker snuggled up tight, flying with Santa Paws through the night.

Before they knew it, they were back in their bed, with dreams of their adventure dancing in their head. Santa Paws patted them, soft and sweet, "Merry Christmas to you, isn't this a treat?"

As the sun peeked up, Christmas Day had begun. Bean and Decker's adventure was over and done. But shh, it's our secret, as they bark with glee, for only you know about their Christmas spree!

And that, Zoom-Arooo Kids, is how Bean and Decker had the best Christmas Eve dash, full of laughter and snowflakes and a magical flash!

Santa Paws Shenanigans: Bean & Decker's Holiday Heist

On the twinkliest, jingliest Christmas morning you ever saw, Bean the Beagle popped open one eye, then the other, and wiggled her nose. She was all set in her jolly red scarf, with Santas that seemed to hop every time she boinged—which was a lot, because Bean was always up to something!

Right next door, on the comfiest doggy bed in the world, Decker the red Cocker Spaniel was snoring away, ears flopped over his eyes like cozy little curtains. His snowflake bow tie looked ready for a fancy party, but Decker? He looked like he wanted five more minutes of dreamy snooze time.

Ping! Clang! Rustle! The house was full of Christmas-y sounds, and smells that would make your tummy grumble for cookies. Everyone was busy, busy, busy—even Uncle Joe, who kept trying to sneak a bit of the yummy ham when he thought no one was watching.

Bean nudged Decker with a wet nose. "Decker, it's playtime!" she yapped in a whispery bark. "Let's make this the most tail-waggingly pawesome Christmas ever!"

Decker's tail thumped, thumped, thumped. That meant, "Okay, but let's sniff out breakfast first!"

Together, they zigzagged around a mountain of gifts and through a jungle of chair legs. They were on a super-duper mission: Operation Yum-Yum. Bean was the brains, and Decker had those puppy-dog eyes that could make anyone go "Awww!"

The family was munching on Christmas lunch when Bean suddenly started singing—well, howling—but it was the most beautiful howl ever. Everyone looked at her, and that's when Decker tiptoed like a ninja and—boop!—nabbed a sausage right off the edge of the table. Ta-da! Mission accomplished! The family couldn't help but giggle, even while they wagged their fingers at the sneaky snack bandits.

Next up: The Mystery of the Sparkly Tree. Every year, Decker wondered if the shiny things hanging on the tree were tasty. And every year, they just tasted like dust. But hope was Decker's middle name (not really, but it should have been).

As Decker eyed a glittery ornament, Bean zoomed in with a "Nuh-uh, not this time!" She had swiped two Santa hats and plopped one onto Decker's head, tilting it just right. Now they looked like Santa's special helpers!

When they pranced into the living room, the whole family burst out laughing so hard that they nearly forgot to open presents!

All day long, Bean led a parade of games, and Decker was so funny that he made everyone's sides ache from chuckling.

As the stars began to twinkle outside, Bean and Decker snuggled up, their eyes twinkling just like the stars. They were sleepy pups, all cuddled and cozy, dreaming of their Christmas capers.

Bean the Beagle and Decker the red Cocker Spaniel had turned a merry Christmas into the waggiest, giggliest day of the year. They weren't just any pups; they were the superstars of Christmas, spreading cheer and belly laughs to everyone they met!

Barks, Baubles, and the Beagle-Spaniel Christmas Boogie!

Oh, jingle jangle, hear that sound?
It's Bean the Beagle, bouncing 'round.
With Decker the Spaniel, red and grand,
They're the merriest pups in all the land!

Deck the halls with barks of holly,
Fa-la-la-la-la, la-la-la-woof!
Bean and Decker's Christmas folly,
Fa-la-la-la-la, la-la-la-roof!

Bean's got a scarf, red and bright,
Decker's bow tie's a festive sight.
They sniff and wag, in Christmas cheer,
Bringing laughs to all who are near!

Deck the halls with barks of holly,
Fa-la-la-la-la, la-la-la-woof!
Bean and Decker's Christmas folly,
Fa-la-la-la-la, la-la-la-roof!

They chase their tails 'round the tree,
Knocking ornaments free with glee.
They howl a tune for the Christmas moon,
Even Santa will be here soon!

Watch them open gifts; it's quite a show,
Ripping paper high and low.
With each surprise, their eyes do gleam,
Every pup's wild Christmas dream!

Deck the halls with barks of holly,
Fa-la-la-la-la, la-la-la-woof!
Bean and Decker, oh so jolly,
Fa-la-la-la-la, la-la-la-roof!

So let's raise a paw, and together sing,
For the joy that Christmas brings.
With Bean and Decker, every girl and boy,
Will find this season full of joy!

WOOF, WOOF!

Thank you so much for diving into the delightful adventures of Bean and Decker with our latest book! We're thrilled you've joined us on this joyous journey. But wait, there's more tail-wagging fun waiting for you! Hop over to **www.walhangroup.co.uk** to explore more exciting tales in the series. Don't miss out on the latest news and exclusive details about the Zoom-Arooo Kids Club. It's a world of adventure, friendship, and endless fun for our little readers!

And here's a special treat just for you: Get your free membership to the Zoom-Arooo Kids Club! Simply visit **https://walhangroup.co.uk/membership-sign-up** and complete the form. Don't forget to use the code Book1317 in the message box to unlock your free membership. Join us now for more amazing stories, activities, and surprises. Let's keep the adventure going! 🌞 🐾 📚

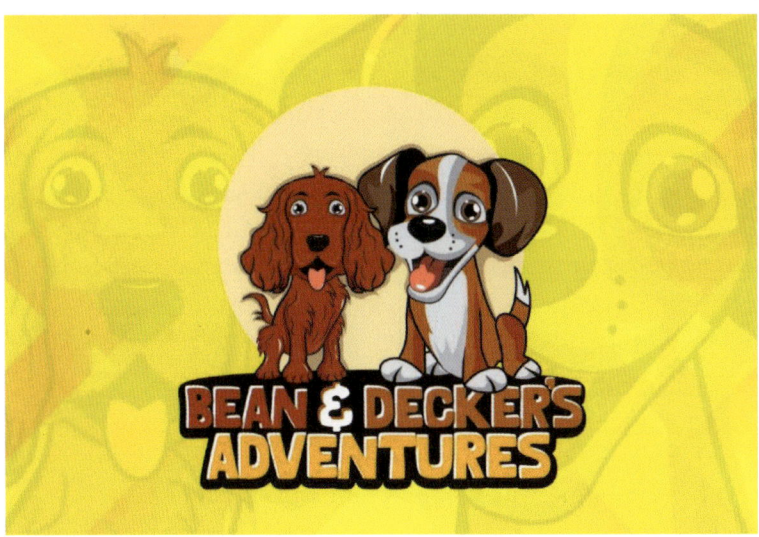

THE END